CHICKEN

CW00591868

CONTENTS

INTRODUCTION

First published in 1997 by
David Bateman Ltd, 30 Tarndale Grove,
Albany, Auckland, New Zealand

Copyright © Allyson Gofton, 1997
Copyright © David Bateman Ltd, 1997

ISBN 1 86953 357 7

Photography Alan Gillard
Design by Errol McLeary
Typeset by TTS Jazz, Auckland
Printed in Hong Kong by Colorcraft Ltd

When I was a child (no, it wasn't that long ago!) chicken was a special treat. But also back then we had Sunday roasts followed by the traditional Sunday drive, and Mickey Mouse was about as exciting as TV got for a child.

Times have certainly changed, and now chicken is as common as hogget was then. It's easy to cook, comes whole, plain or seasoned, is pre-cut into selected portions for us to use for different dishes, or can be purchased pre-cooked with or without stuffing. Chicken can be cooked any way you like and the ideas are endless. This book has some of my favourite chicken recipes.

Chicken must be well cooked. This is particularly so if you are eating portions on the bone. To test whether a whole chicken is cooked, pierce through the meat between the leg and thigh bones and see if the juices run clear. If they are pink the chicken requires further cooking. If the juices are clear the bird is cooked. When reheating portions, especially drumsticks or wings, these too must be reheated right through to the bone to prevent any worry of catching bugs. This thorough cooking cannot be stressed enough.

Never prepare raw chicken (or meat) on a chopping board and then place cooked chicken (or meat) on top of the board without first thoroughly washing the board. This is a perfect recipe for an upset tummy. Between these steps, wash the board well in hot soapy water.

Unfortunately today, supermarkets offer little service and you have to ask to have frozen and chilled foods wrapped. It is always best to have chicken pieces (and other meats) wrapped to insulate them. It is better still to have a chilly bin in the car with iced bricks if you are not going directly home after shopping. Bugs breed at an alarming rate once chilled food warms.

Chicken is a wonderful family meal choice. While it is now readily available, I believe the flavour has been sacrificed to meet market demands. If you can find free-range chickens do use them as the flavour is quite wonderful.

I hope you will enjoy this somewhat eclectic collection of my favourite ways with chicken.

Cook's Tip

If you'd like the soup thicker blend 2 tsp cornflour with a little water and stir in just before serving. Do not boil once thickened or the soup will become thin again.

CHICKEN NOODLE AND CRAB SOUP

2 x 26 g packets chicken noodle
    soup
4 cups (1 litre) water
2 eggs, well beaten
100 g surimi, finely shredded*
¹/₂ cup cooked chicken meat,
    shredded (optional), fresh or
    smoked
2 spring onions, finely sliced
425 g can creamed corn
Pepper to season

This Asian favourite can be made quickly using good old Chicken Noodle Soup.

1. Empty the contents of the packets into a large saucepan and add the water. Bring to the boil. Simmer 5 minutes.

2. Gradually pour the beaten eggs into the soup, stirring constantly so the eggs form lots of strings.

3. Add the surimi, chicken, spring onions, corn and season with pepper. Simmer 1 minute.

Serve in bowls garnished with a sprig of coriander or parsley and a little chopped red pepper or chilli.

Serves 4

* Surimi is the man-made crab meat available in the supermarkets, either sliced or in stick form. Use canned or fresh crab meat if wished.

SMOKED CHICKEN AND VEGETABLE CHOWDER

50 g butter

1 onion, peeled and finely
    chopped

1 carrot, peeled and finely
    chopped

1 large potato, peeled and finely
    chopped

3 stalks celery, peeled and finely
    chopped

3 tblsp flour

2 cups chicken stock

1 double breast smoked chicken,
    skin removed

2 cups milk

$1/4$ cup each chopped parsley
    and celery leaves (optional)

Wonderful in winter, served with hot bread rolls or freshly baked cheese scones. The celery leaves give a lovely flavour to the soup; add them just at the end. Oh! and served with hot cheese muffins the chowder is a great meal.

1. Heat the butter in a large saucepan and add the onion, carrot, potato and celery, stirring well to coat in the butter. Lower heat, cover and cook for 10 minutes.

2. Stir in the flour and cook for 1 minute.

3. Gradually stir in the stock and continue stirring until thickened. Cover and simmer for 5 minutes.

4. Dice the smoked chicken and add to the soup with the milk, parsley and celery leaves. Bring to a simmer. Season with pepper if wished.

Serves 4–6

Cook's Tip

A chowder takes its name
from the French cooking
vessel in which a hearty
soup was cooked by
fishermen. The word
'chaudiere' now means a
hearty, chunky soup.

WARM ROAST CHICKEN AND PEACH SALAD
with a Roasted Garlic and Yoghurt Dressing

1 whole chicken (unseasoned)
Salt and pepper to season
A little oil (preferably olive)
1 bulb garlic
400 g can sliced peaches (well
    drained), or 2 fresh peaches
    stoned and sliced
1 bunch asparagus
Lettuce for 6 (use a combination
    of green, red and bitter)
Small handful chopped fresh
    chives or parsley
1 cup sprouts (bean, mung,
    snow pea)

Dressing
Garlic (as above)
1/4 cup oil (preferably olive)
1/4 cup cider vinegar
1/2 cup non-fat plain yoghurt
1/4 cup chopped fresh tarragon or
    1 tblsp dried
Salt, pepper and a pinch sugar
Squeeze of lemon juice

Flavours of peach and chicken go together well with a tarragon and garlic dressing — ideal for summer entertaining.

1. Wash the chicken, dry with absorbent paper and place on a roasting tray. Season with salt and pepper and rub skin with a little oil. Wrap garlic in foil and place both chicken and garlic into oven. Roast at 180°C for 60–70 minutes until chicken is cooked. The garlic will be cooked as well.
2. Cut any larger peach slices in half.
3. Blanch the asparagus and cut the spears in half crosswise.
4. Tear meat from the bones and cut into chunky pieces. Leave skin on or off as wished.
5. Toss the chicken, peaches, asparagus, lettuce, chives or parsley and sprouts together in the dressing and serve immediately. The chicken should still be warm.

Serves 6

Dressing
Cut the cooked garlic in half horizontally and squeeze cloves into a bowl. Add the remaining ingredients and whisk until thick. Season well with salt, pepper, sugar and lemon juice.

8

Time Saver Tip

Use a rotisserie chicken
from the supermarket,
preferably without
stuffing. They're already
cooked, but make sure
you use it quickly on
reaching home, otherwise
refrigerate and have cold
in the salad.

SUMMER MELON AND SMOKED CHICKEN SALAD

*4 juicy ripe large outdoor
    tomatoes*
1 cantaloupe melon
1 honeydew melon
2 avocados
1 breast smoked chicken

Basil Vinaigrette
³/₄ cup vinaigrette (see Note)
*¼ cup chopped fresh basil or
    1 tblsp dried sweet basil*

This salad is a delicate combination of fruits. Juicy fresh melons with plenty of flavour are needed. The dressing of basil vinaigrette is delicious and different. Remove the salad from the fridge about ³/₄ hour before serving as anything too cold has no flavour.

1. Blanch the tomatoes and refresh in cold water. Remove the skin. Cut into quarters.
2. Halve the cantaloupe and honeydew melons and scoop out the seeds. Ball the melons or remove the skin and dice into 2 cm pieces.
3. Peel and slice the avocados into 1 cm slices.
4. Remove the skin from the smoked chicken and cut into slices.
5. Toss together the tomatoes, melons, avocados and smoked chicken.

Pour over the basil dressing and serve from a large bowl or on top of a lettuce-lined plate.

Serves 4 as main course

Basil Vinaigrette

In a food processor mix together the vinaigrette and basil. If using fresh basil make the dressing just before serving as the basil will brown if allowed to stand.

Note

A basic vinaigrette can be made from 3 parts oil (preferably olive) to 1 part vinegar (preferably wine or cider), a good seasoning of salt and pepper, a squeeze of lemon juice and a dash of prepared mustard. Blend well, store in a sealed jar in the refrigerator and bring to room temperature before serving.

Cook's Tip

Flavours that go well
with chicken include
garlic; herbs, especially
thyme, chives, parsley
and rosemary; all good
things Mediterranean,
like olives, capers,
anchovies; nuts,
especially walnuts,
cashews; cumin; yoghurt;
coriander, fresh & dried;
Asian flavours of ginger,
soy & hoisin sauces,
chillies, coconut;
mustards & honeys.
There's a bounty of
partners just waiting.

Asian Chicken Liver Pâté

ASIAN CHICKEN LIVER PÂTÉ

25 g butter
1 small onion, peeled and finely
    chopped
2 tsp finely chopped fresh ginger
250 g chicken livers
2 tsp ground cumin
2 tblsp dry sherry
2 tblsp cream
Salt and pepper to season

Chicken pâté is so quick to prepare and with a little bit of added spice, it's far better than the heavy gelatin-glazed supermarket versions.

1. Heat the butter in a frying pan and add the onion and ginger. Cook over a moderate heat until the onion has softened but is not coloured.
2. Trim the livers of the core and cut in half. Add the livers and cumin to the pan and cook, tossing over a moderate heat until the livers are almost cooked. Add the sherry and cream and bring to the boil for one minute.
3. Transfer the contents of the pan to a food processor and process until smooth. Season with salt and pepper to taste.
4. Transfer to a serving dish. Refrigerate, covered, until well chilled.

Serve garnished with coriander or parsley and cashews.

Makes about 1 1/2 cups

SMOKED CHICKEN PÂTÉ

1/2 breast smoked chicken, skin
    removed, chopped
125 g cream cheese
1 spring onion, trimmed of most
    of the green
2 tblsp dry sherry

1. In a food processor put the chopped smoked chicken, cream cheese, spring onion and sherry. Process until the mixture is smooth.
2. Transfer to a serving dish and serve with crackers or mini toasts. Garnish with sprigs of parsley if wished.

Makes about 1 1/2 cups

CAJUN NIBBLES WITH SPICY SAUCE

1 kg chicken wings
3 tblsp Paul Prudhomme's Poultry
    Magic
½ cup white wine or orange juice

Spicy Sauce
6 spring onions, trimmed
2 cloves garlic, crushed, peeled
    and mashed to a paste
2 cm piece root ginger, peeled
1 tblsp brown sugar
1 orange, peeled to remove rind
    and skin
1 tsp each ground allspice, white
    pepper and cinnamon
½ tsp each ground nutmeg and
    cayenne
2 tblsp chopped fresh thyme or
    2 tsp dried
½ cup each freshly squeezed
    orange juice and white wine
    vinegar
2 tblsp dark soy sauce or
    Indonesian Ketjap Manis
2 tblsp oil (preferably olive)

This recipe makes good use of the pre-made seasonings from Lousianna chef, Paul Prudhomme. Just dust the wings with "Magic" and grill. I've added a little wine for more taste. The spicy sauce can be made in advance, but needs whizzing before being served.

1. Trim the chicken wings, remove and discard the tips and cut the wings in half. Mix the Poultry Magic and wine or orange juice together in a lidded container and toss in the chicken wings. Cover and marinate overnight or for about 4 hours.

2. Heat the grill of an oven to about 200°C. If you have a fan grill this is 180°C.

3. Arrange the chicken nibbles on a rack and grill at the top of the oven for about 15 minutes or until the chicken nibbles are golden. Turn occasionally during cooking.

Serve in a large basket with the spicy sauce.

Makes about 20.

Spicy Sauce
Put all the ingredients except the oil into a food processor and process until the mixture is well blended. With the motor running pour the oil down the feed tube until it is well mixed in. If wished, garnish with orange rind and slivers of spring onion.

Note

This sauce is particularly
nice when first made.

Cook's Tip

Spices are best kept in
airtight containers away
from direct sunlight to
ensure that they keep
their fabulous flavours.

SHERRY COATED CHICKEN BALLS

½ x 225 g can bamboo shoots,
    well drained
½ x 230 g can water chestnuts,
    well drained
50 g mushrooms
2 cloves garlic, crushed, peeled
    and mashed to a paste
200 g each of chicken and pork
    mince
1 tblsp dark soy sauce
2 tblsp chilli sauce
1 egg
2 tblsp chopped fresh coriander or
    parsley

Sauce
½ cup medium sherry
¼ cup brown sugar
1 tblsp minced ginger
1 tblsp each plum and dark soy
    sauce
Pinch chilli powder
1 tsp cornflour

Bamboo shoots and water chestnuts give these meatballs both flavour and texture. They can be made in advance and reheated in the microwave before serving. Serve them with toothpicks.

1. In a food processor put the bamboo shoots, water chestnuts, mushrooms and garlic and process until the mixture is finely chopped.
2. Add the mince meats, sauces, egg, coriander or parsley and pulse only until the mixture is mixed.
3. Roll tablespoonful lots into balls. Pan fry the balls in a little oil until golden and cooked. Drain on absorbent paper.
4. In a large frying pan put the sherry, brown sugar, ginger, plum and soy sauces and chilli powder and bring to the boil. Mix the cornflour with a little water to make a smooth paste and pour into the sauce ingredients. Stir over a moderate heat until thickened. Add the meatballs and toss in the sauce. Transfer to a large serving dish. Garnish with chopped spring onions and toasted sesame seeds.

Makes 24

Note
The meatballs can be reheated in the sauce. Do not boil too long as the sauce will break down and become thin.

Cook's Tip

Use a small chopping
board for garlic only.
Garlic is very pungent
and will taint chopping
boards. Keeping a
separate garlic board
avoids having your
sandwiches or next slice
of cake hinting of garlic.

Cook's Tip

Home-made chicken
stock is always
preferable. If you do not
have any on hand here
are some alternatives:
* Chicken stock powder:
use 1 tsp per cup water.
* Tetra Pak Chicken
Stock: dilute with equal
quantities of water.
For a home-made chicken
stock recipe, see page 48.

SMOKED CHICKEN AND PUMPKIN SAUCE ON PASTA

*1 double breast smoked chicken,
   skin removed*
1 tblsp oil (preferably olive)
*3 spring onions, trimmed and
   finely chopped*
*2 cloves garlic, crushed, peeled
   and mashed to a paste*
2 cups pumpkin puree*
2 cups chicken stock
1 cup fresh or frozen peas
*2 tblsp chopped fresh basil or
   1 tblsp dried*
Salt and pepper to season
Spaghetti or fettuccine for four
Parmesan cheese to serve

Pumpkin makes a wonderful sauce to accompany pasta.

1. Slice the smoked chicken breast in half and slice each half into thin strips.

2. Heat the oil in a frying pan and cook the spring onion and garlic for about 2–3 minutes until fragrant. Add the pumpkin purée and chicken stock and simmer for 5 minutes.

3. Add the smoked chicken, peas and basil. Season with salt and pepper.

4. Serve the sauce over freshly cooked pasta and have the Parmesan cheese on the side.

Serves 4–6

* Steam or microwave pumpkin until soft, then puree or mash well. Depending on the type of pumpkin, you will achieve varying results with the purée — maybe thicker or thinner. Add the stock with a little caution to achieve a smooth sauce that will coat the pasta and be neither too thick nor too thin.

CHICKEN WITH FRESH TOMATOES AND HERBS

2 double chicken breasts, skin
  removed
4 bacon rashers, rind removed
2 tblsp oil (preferably olive)
2 stalks celery, finely sliced
6 spring onions, trimmed and
  finely sliced
2 cloves garlic, crushed, peeled
  and mashed to a paste
4 tomatoes, blanched and finely
  diced
6 leaves basil or 1 tsp dried
1/4 cup chopped parsley or
  1 tblsp dried
1/4 cup chicken stock or white
  wine
Salt and pepper to season
Spaghetti for 6
Parmesan cheese to serve

Freshness of flavours is the key here, making this a lovely way of enjoying chicken and pasta in summer.

1. Finely slice the chicken breast and bacon rashers.

2. Heat the oil in a frying pan and cook the chicken and bacon over a high heat tossing until browned and half cooked.

3. Add the celery, spring onions and garlic and cook a further 2 minutes.

4. Toss in the tomatoes, basil, parsley and stock or wine. Stir well and season with salt and pepper.

5. Have pasta cooked and well drained. Toss chicken through pasta and serve with the Parmesan cheese on the side.

Serves 6

Cook's Tip

Salt either comes from
the sea or is mined from
beneath the earth's
surface. There are many
different types of salt
now available (sea, rock,
kosher, etc), but they are
all salt and we shouldn't
have too much. However,
salt does bring out the
flavour in food and a
pinch is still okay.

MUSHROOM AND CHICKEN STUFFED PASTA SHELLS

16 large pasta shells
2 tblsp oil (preferably olive)
1 small onion, peeled and finely
  chopped
250 g chicken mince
4 large (250 g) flat mushrooms
1/2 cup sour cream
Salt and pepper to season

Cheese Sauce
25 g butter
2 tblsp flour
1³/₄ cups milk
1 cup grated fresh Parmesan or
  Cheddar cheese

Rich and yummy. For a truly delicious mushroom flavour, use field (flat) mushrooms or gourmet browns.

1. Cook the pasta shells in plenty of boiling salted water until al dente. Drain and place into a well-greased, shallow baking dish. The dish should be just large enough to hold the shells comfortably. Cover with plastic wrap and set aside.
2. Heat the oil in a frying pan and add the onion and chicken mince and fry over a moderately high heat, breaking up the mince with a fork as you go.
3. Finely chop the mushrooms. Add to the chicken and toss for about 2 minutes over a moderate heat. Add sour cream and simmer for 2 minutes. Season with salt and pepper.
4. Spoon the filling into the shells. Pour the cheese sauce over the shells. Sprinkle with remaining cheese.
5. Bake at 200°C for 15 minutes and then grill for a few minutes until golden. Serve with plenty of vegetables or crisp green salad.

Serves 4–6

Cheese Sauce
Melt butter in a saucepan and stir in flour. Cook 1–2 minutes over a moderate heat until frothy. Gradually stir in the milk and continue to stir until the sauce has thickened. Stir in ³/₄ of the cheese, reserving the remainder as a topping. Season with salt and pepper.

Cook's Tip

If you cannot find large
pasta shells, then use
cannelloni tubes and
they'll work just fine.
'Al dente' is an Italian
phrase for 'to the tooth'
and is used to describe
pasta or other foods that
are cooked until they
offer a little resistance
when bitten into, but
are neither too soft nor
too hard.

CHICKEN LIVERS WITH CASHEWS

400 g chicken livers
2 carrots, peeled
50 g snow peas, trimmed
1 tblsp oil (preferably olive)
1 clove garlic, crushed, peeled
    and mashed to a paste
2 cm piece ginger, peeled
1 tblsp light soy sauce
1 tblsp sweet chilli sauce
½ tsp cornflour
¼ cup chicken stock or water
70 g packet cashew nut pieces,
    lightly toasted

The texture combinations make this dish especially delicious.

1. Trim the chicken livers of any sinew and core parts and cut each in half. Cut the carrots into matchsticks. Cook the carrots and the snow peas in boiling water for 2 minutes. Drain and set aside.

2. Heat the oil in a frying pan to moderately hot. Add chicken livers and cook quickly until brown on the outside and a little pink inside. Stir in the garlic and ginger.

3. Combine the soy sauce, chilli sauce, cornflour and chicken stock or water. Add to the pan along with cashews, carrots and snow peas. Simmer for 1–2 minutes. Serve with white rice and salad greens.

Serves 4

Cook's Tip

Chinese soy sauce comes
in two grades, light
(white) or dark (black).
The light one is great for
serving at the table,
while the dark is ideal
for marinades but should
be used with caution.
There is also Tamari and
Shoyu, Japanese soy
sauces which are best
used for Japanese
cooking. Ketjap Manis is
Indonesian soy sauce and
is much thicker, darker
and sweeter and adds a
wonderful flavour to
Oriental foods.

Cook's Tip

When cooking dishes with a pastry base, I like to place them into the oven on top of a preheated baking tray. The instant heat helps to cook the base of the pie.

CHICKEN AND HAM PIE

4 chicken leg and thigh portions
200 g ham, finely shredded
2 tblsp mustard (your
   preference)
½ cup cream (fresh or sour
   cream)
3 spring onions, finely chopped
Salt and pepper to season
3 sheets pre-rolled puff pastry,
   defrosted
Milk to glaze

This pie looks like it took more trouble to make than it did. It is ideal on picnics in summer, on cold winter nights, or anything in between.

1. Poach the leg and thigh portions in about 2½–3 cups water for 40–50 minutes or until tender. Remove from stock and cool. (Stock can be kept for other dishes if wished.)

2. When cool, remove skin and pull meat from bones. Flake the meat into a bowl and mix in the ham, mustard, cream and spring onions. Season with salt and pepper.

3. Take one pastry sheet and place on a greased baking tray. Arrange the chicken and ham filling in the centre leaving a 1 cm edge all the way around. Brush the pastry edge with milk.

4. Roll the remaining 2 sheets together to form a larger square about 28 cm square.

5. Fold the square in half. With a floured knife and leaving a 5 cm border all the way round, cut at right angles to the fold at 2 cm intervals. Open the pastry out. You should have many slices in the centre of the square.

6. Arrange the pastry over the top of the chicken pie, pressing down the edges. Brush the whole pastry top with milk to glaze.

7. Bake at 240°C (220° fan bake) at the top of the oven for 20 minutes, or until hot and golden.

Serves 6

THYME BAKED CHICKEN WITH PRUNES AND OLIVES

1 onion, peeled and diced
8–10 boneless chicken thigh
    portions
16 pitted prunes
16 stuffed olives
3–4 sprigs fresh thyme or ½ tsp
    dried
½ tsp ground black pepper
Pinch of salt
¾ cup chicken stock
¼ cup medium sherry*

Being entertained by fellow colleagues is always a treat and Sue Lyons, Food Editor of *Woman's Day*, introduced me to the olive and prune combination with chicken one evening. I was hooked and have tried hard to recreate that dish here. It was simply delicious served with fluffy white rice and a crisp green salad.

1. Sprinkle the onion over the base of a 4 cup (1 litre) capacity oven dish.

2. Roll chicken thighs and arrange neatly on top. Sprinkle over the prunes, olives, thyme, pepper and salt.

3. Pour the stock and sherry in and cover with a lid or foil.

4. Bake at 190°C for 50 minutes. Serve on plain boiled rice with green vegetables.

Serves 4

* If you don't have medium dry sherry, use chicken stock or white wine, it's just that sherry and olives are perfect partners.

Cook's Tip

You can add a bit of extra heat to this dish by using marinated stuffed green olives, available in supermarkets bottled or sold loose at the delicatessen.

CHICKEN AND ASPARAGUS BAKE
with Cheese Crumble

4 chicken leg and thigh portions
1 onion, peeled and diced
2 cloves garlic, crushed, peeled
    and mashed to a paste
    (optional)
50 g butter
4 tblsp flour
1½ cups chicken stock
¼ cup cream
¼ cup chopped parsley or 1
    tblsp dried
340 g can asparagus pieces, well
    drained
Salt and pepper to season

Crumble Topping

4 slices of toast bread (white or
    wholemeal)
25 g butter
¼ cup grated Cheddar or Edam
    cheese

My mother's favourite chicken partner is asparagus. I've combined both these ingredients here with a savoury crumble topping which is quick to make and adds a crunchy texture.

1. Place leg and thigh portions in a large saucepan or lidded frying pan. Cover with about 2½–3 cups water and bring to a simmer for 40–50 minutes until cooked. Remove from stock and cool.
2. In a medium-sized saucepan cook the onion and garlic in the butter over a low to moderate heat for about 5–7 minutes until the onion has softened.
3. Add the flour and cook stirring for 1 minute. Gradually stir in the chicken stock and keep stirring until the sauce thickens. Cook a further 2–3 minutes before stirring in the cream, parsley and asparagus. Remove from the heat and season with salt and pepper.
4. Pull the meat from the chicken bones discarding fat. Fold the chicken into the sauce and spread into a 4 cup capacity oven dish. Sprinkle over the crumble topping.
5. Bake at 190°C for 30 minutes until piping hot and golden.

Serves 4. Serve with seasonal vegetables.

Crumble Topping

Process the bread to crumbs in a food processor or crumble by rubbing between your hands. Rub in butter and stir through grated cheese.

Cook's Tip

When opening a can of asparagus spears, open the can upside down and then empty out the contents into a sieve to drain. This way you will not damage the delicate asparagus tips.

Cook's Tip

When you prepare a chicken this way it is easy to cut it into four portions for serving. Remove the thigh and leg joint by lifting and cutting through the skin. Cut down either side of the breast bone and lift away the breast meat.

CHICKEN WITH APRICOT AND HONEY MUSTARD

1 whole chicken (unseasoned)

Apricot and Honey Mustard
8 plump dried apricots
4 tblsp honey
1 x 175 g jar Mild English or
*   American Mustard*

The honey butter stuffing makes this quick chicken dish special. If you don't have time to remove the backbone from the chicken, ask your butcher to do it. Butchers at the supermarket are usually happy to help.

1. Wash and pat dry the chicken. Using kitchen scissors or a sharp knife cut down either side of the backbone and remove it.
2. Place the chicken breast side up on a board and press down gently to flatten. Use your fingers to separate the skin from the meat.
3. Spread about $1/4$ of the apricot and honey mustard between the skin and meat on both the breasts, leg and thigh joints.
4. Place the chicken on a rack above a baking dish. Place on the second lowest rack from the bottom and fan grill at 160°C for $1^1/4$–$1^1/2$ hours until the chicken is cooked.

I like to cook chicken this way occasionally as it gives a crispy skin and moist meat. Don't use a standard grill as this will burn the chicken without cooking. If you don't have a fan grill option, fan bake at 160°C for 1–$1^1/4$ hours. If you don't have a fan bake, bake at 180°C for 1–$1^1/4$ hours or until cooked. Serve the chicken with fresh vegetables and the remaining apricot and honey mustard.

Serves 4

Apricot and Honey Mustard
Place apricots, honey and mustard into a food processor and process for about 3–4 minutes until smooth. If wished, season with fresh herbs like rosemary, chives or parsley.

BAKED CHICKEN UNDER A POTATO CRUST

*4–6 slices bacon, trimmed of
  rind*
*8–10 boneless chicken thigh
  portions (skin removed)*
¼ cup seasoned flour
2 tblsp oil (preferably olive)
1 kg potatoes
*½ tsp each dried thyme and
  dried tarragon*
*2 large onions, peeled and
  chopped*
*4 cloves garlic, crushed, peeled
  and mashed to a paste*
2 cups chicken stock
25 g butter, melted
Freshly ground black pepper

This is a great winter casserole, ideal with plenty of winter vegetables.

1. Dice the bacon and cut the chicken portions in half. Toss the chicken in the seasoned flour. Heat the oil and pan-fry the chicken and bacon over a moderate heat for 10 minutes until the chicken is golden.

2. Wash (do not peel) and slice the potatoes into 0.5 cm thick slices and arrange half the slices in the bottom of a deep casserole.

3. Top with the bacon, chicken, herbs, onions and garlic.

4. Layer the remaining potatoes on top.

5. Pour over the stock. Brush the melted butter on top of the potatoes. Season well with pepper.

6. Bake at 160°C for about 1¼–1½ hours or until tender. Add more stock if required.

Serves 4

If wished, grill the potato topping for 1–2 minutes before serving to brown and crisp a little more.

Cook's Tip

Pepper is an essential
ingredient in our
kitchens. There are 3
types to use. Black
peppercorns have the
strongest flavour with a
touch of sweetness.
White peppercorns have
a milder flavour and
their colour makes them
perfect for seasoning
white sauces. Green
peppercorns are more
spicy than hot.

SPICY YOGHURT BAKED CHICKEN DRUMSTICKS

8 chicken drumsticks
2 spring onions, trimmed and
    finely chopped
2 tblsp fruit chutney
1 tsp each ground ginger and
    garam masala
2 tblsp honey
½ cup natural unsweetened
    yoghurt

Sweet flavours of fruit chutney and spices bring these chicken drumsticks to life.

1. Remove and discard the skin from the drumsticks if wished. Place drumsticks into a shallow lidded container.

2. In a bowl blend together the spring onions, chutney, ginger, garam masala, honey and yoghurt. Pour the yoghurt mix over the drumsticks and turn to coat well.

3. Cover and refrigerate for 2–3 hours, or leave overnight. The longer you leave the chicken, the more intense the flavour.

4. Bake at 180°C for 35–40 minutes until the legs are well cooked.

Serve hot or cold.

Serves 4

Note
Other portions like 4 chicken breast portions or 4 chicken leg and thigh portions can also be used as a change.

Cook's Tip

If you plan to cook these on the BBQ then brush off any excess marinade before barbecuing to prevent burning.

Removing the skin from chicken also assists in removing the excess fat which adheres to the chicken skin.

Cook's Tip

When you substitute fresh herbs with dried, work to a ratio of half the amount dried to fresh. With strong flavoured herbs like rosemary you can use quarter to fresh.

WHOLE BAKED CHICKEN MADE EASY

1 whole chicken (unseasoned)
2 tblsp oil (preferably olive)
3–4 large cloves garlic, crushed,
*   peeled and roughly chopped*
1 branch fresh rosemary
Flour for dusting
A little butter for dotting

I still maintain that a roast chicken is one of the easiest ways to prepare chicken. Once it's in the oven, there's no work to do. This is how I cook a roast chicken in my home.

1. Using kitchen scissors or a sharp knife cut the chicken down either side of the backbone. Remove and discard the backbone section or use to make stock. Place chicken on chopping board and firmly press out flat.
2. Heat the oil in an ovenproof frying pan, large enough to hold the chicken. Add the garlic and rosemary and cook for one minute.
3. Add the chicken breast side up and sprinkle heavily with flour. Dot with the butter.
4. Bake 180°C for about 1–1$\frac{1}{4}$ hours or until chicken is cooked. Baste occasionally with any pan juices.
   Serve with roasted red peppers, kumara and onions.

Serves 4

Roasted Red Peppers
Grill 2 red peppers under a very high heat until skin is blackened all over. Place in a plastic bag and leave to cool thoroughly. Peel away the charred skin, core and cut into quarters. Drizzle with a little olive oil and sprinkle with salt.

SWEET 'N' SOUR GLAZED DRUMSTICKS

½ cup brown sugar
½ cup white wine vinegar
¼ cup pineapple or orange juice
1 tblsp tomato paste or tomato
    sauce
½ tsp each ground ginger and
    five spice powder
1 clove garlic, crushed, peeled
    and mashed to a paste
8 chicken drumsticks

These drumsticks are great cold on a picnic.

1. Put the brown sugar, vinegar, pineapple or orange juice, tomato paste, spices and garlic into a saucepan and boil for 2 minutes stirring constantly. Cool.

2. Remove the skin from chicken drumsticks if wished and place in a shallow lidded container.

3. Pour over the sweet and sour marinade and toss well to coat. Cover and refrigerate for 4 hours or overnight. The longer the chicken marinates, the more intense the flavour.

4. BBQ or grill with a moderate heat for about 20 minutes until cooked or bake at 180°C for 30–35 minutes. Brush any remaining marinade over drumsticks as they cook.

Serves 4

Note
As the marinade has a lot of sweetness (sugar, pineapple or orange juice, tomato paste), be careful when cooking the drumsticks over the BBQ, as they will burn easily.

Cook's Tip

Wine vinegar is made, as the name suggests, from wine and is much more subtle than white vinegar which is distilled malt vinegar. I prefer wine or cider as they will not leave that harsh sharpness in the dish.

Cook's Tip

Never boil anything that
includes yoghurt,
otherwise the yoghurt
can curdle. Just bring to
a warm heat without
boiling.

CHICKEN AND CASHEW NUT CURRY

2 tblsp butter (preferably
    unsalted)
2 tblsp oil (preferably olive)
1.5 kg (about 12) chicken thigh
    portions, skin removed
2 onions, peeled and sliced
4 large juicy cloves garlic,
    crushed, peeled and mashed
    to a paste
1 tblsp finely chopped fresh
    ginger
$1/2$ tsp each chilli powder, ground
    coriander, cloves and cumin
1 tsp turmeric
$1^1/2$ tblsp flour
3 cups chicken stock
2 x 70 g packets cashews,
    roasted
Salt and pepper to season
1–2 tblsp yoghurt to accompany
Fresh coriander to garnish

This is one of the nicest curries I think I have ever made. The gentle flavour of the spices with roasted cashews is just magic.

1. Heat the butter and oil in a large frying pan, add the chicken pieces and brown well on all sides. Transfer to a plate.

2. Add the onion, garlic and ginger to the pan with all the spices and allow the mixture to cook for about 3–4 minutes over a moderate heat until the pan smells wonderfully fragrant. Stir regularly.

3. Add the flour and cook a further minute. Stir in the chicken stock and bring to the boil. Simmer for 10 minutes. Return the chicken to the pan and cook for about 30–35 minutes until the pieces are well cooked.

4. Take $2/3$ of the cashews and process them in a blender or food processor until finely chopped but not a powder. Add to the pan with the remaining whole cashews. Season with salt and pepper.

5. Garnish with the yoghurt and fresh coriander before serving with plenty of rice.

Serves 6–8

CHICKEN IN RED WINE WITH MUSHROOMS

*4 chicken leg and thigh portions,
    skin removed*
2 tblsp flour
2 tblsp oil (preferably olive)
*2 onions, peeled and roughly
    chopped*
½ cup tomato paste
1 cup red wine
1 cup chicken stock
8 flat mushrooms
Salt and pepper to season

This is an easy-to-make winter casserole that's just a bit special.

1. Dust the chicken pieces in the flour (reserving any left-over flour). Heat the oil in a frying pan and add pieces to the pan. Cook over a moderately high heat for 5 minutes to brown chicken on all sides.

2. Transfer pieces to a casserole. Return the pan to the heat and add the onion. Cook 3–4 minutes stirring regularly until the onion has browned and softened.

3. Add the tomato paste and cook a further 3–4 minutes, stirring regularly until the tomato paste becomes a very dark brown/red colour. Sprinkle over any remaining flour and stir in.

4. Gradually stir in the red wine and stock. Bring to the boil and pour over the chicken. Place the mushrooms on top.

5. Cover and bake at 180°C for 50–60 minutes or until the chicken pieces are tender. Season with salt and pepper.

Serve with plenty of mashed potatoes and green vegetables.

Serves 4

Cook's Tip

Always use a reasonably
good quality wine to cook
with. If the wine is not
good enough to drink, it
will be worse heated and
will ruin your dish.

SUMMER CHICKEN

4 chicken leg and thigh portions
¼ cup chopped fresh herbs
    (parsley, chives or thyme)
2 tblsp honey
Grated rind one lemon
2 tblsp butter
Pepper to season

Hugely successful. It's one of the easiest ways to prepare chicken leg and thigh portions.

1. Carefully rub your thumb or finger between the skin and the meat on the chicken leg and thigh portions to release the skin from the meat.

2. In a bowl mix together the chopped herbs, honey, lemon rind and butter and season well with pepper.

3. Place ¼ of this mixture under the skin of each chicken portion, pressing down firmly with the hand to ensure that the filling spreads out along the chicken and the skin covers the chicken.

4. Place the chicken portions on a rack above a baking dish. Bake at 180°C for 50–60 minutes until the portions are well cooked. Depending on the size of the portions it may take the full 60 minutes.

To test if cooked, pierce the meat with a skewer at the thickest part of the portion. The juice should be clear; if still pink return to the oven for a further 5 minutes and test again.

Serves 4

Cook's Tip

If you wish you can remove the skin after cooking. The flavours from the stuffing will have oozed their way through the chicken meat.

CHICKEN STOCK

1 kg chicken bones
3 litres (12 cups) water
1 carrot, peeled and roughly
    chopped
1 onion, peeled and roughly
    chopped
1 stalk celery, trimmed and
    roughly chopped
1/2 leek, well washed and
    roughly chopped (optional)
1 bouquet garni*
1 tblsp peppercorns

Basic chicken stock can now be purchased in the supermarkets, sold by the Good Taste Company. However, it's cheaper to make at home, takes little effort and you can add variations as listed to match whatever you're cooking.

1. Wash the bones to remove any blood. Place them in a large stock pot and cover with the water and bring to the boil.

2. Add the vegetables, bouquet garni and peppercorns and simmer gently, uncovered, preferably for 3 hours. Strain and cool quickly.

Store covered in the refrigerator.

Makes around 2 litres.

* Bouquet garni is made from one bay leaf, a few sprigs fresh thyme and a few stalks parsley wrapped together with string. If you do not have these ingredients you can leave them out, though the stock will lack that subtle herb flavour.

Variations
While the classics would use the above style of recipe only I always think it's nice to add some flavours of the foods you are cooking with, such as:

* Lemon grass and ginger for Thai foods * Star anise for Chinese foods * Cinnamon stick and cloves for Indian foods * Plenty of fresh parsley and squashed tomatoes for Italian foods